Live Music!

Keyboards

Elizabeth Sharma

Thomson Learning
New York

Books in the series

Brass   Strings
Keyboards   The Voice
Percussion   Woodwinds

First published in the
United States in 1993 by
Thomson Learning
115 Fifth Avenue
New York, NY 10003

First published in 1993 by
Wayland (Publishers) Ltd

Cataloging-in-Publication Data applied for

ISBN: 1-56847-117-3

Printed in Italy

Contents

Words printed in **dark type** are explained
in the glossary.

It's all there in black and white

Have you ever run your fingers all the way up and down a piano keyboard? Maybe you have played an electronic keyboard instrument.

There are many instruments, such as the harpsichord, organ, and accordion, with keys arranged in the same way as a piano keyboard. If you know how to play a tune on one, you can play it on all of them.

The musician in the middle is playing an electronic keyboard in a band. He can produce many exciting sounds on it.

It's very easy to make a pleasant sound on a keyboard. You can play several notes at the same time. With practice, you will learn to play the **melody** and the **accompaniment** together.

This girl is trying to make a good sound on the keyboards.

Do you play the soft-loud?

A good pianist can play sweet, slow music, making the notes sing. Pianists can also make their fingers move very fast to create a rippling sound. Groups of notes can be played together to form full, rich **chords**.

The piano can be used to play quiet accompaniments for **solo** singers, or to play jazz, blues, or popular music. It can be played loudly or very softly. That is why its full name is pianoforte. It means "soft-loud" in Italian.

Fats Domino is a wonderful jazz pianist. His nimble fingers ripple up and down the piano.

A piano is like a harp in a box. The metal strings are stretched across a frame. They are struck with padded hammers instead of being plucked like harp strings.

Look inside a grand piano while you press on one of the keys. Can you see what happens?

When you press a key, a pad called a damper is lifted from the string. A hammer strikes the string. When the key is released, the damper comes down again. The damper keeps the string from vibrating and echoing, so that notes played one after the other do not sound blurred together.

Now look at the strings for the high notes and the strings for the low notes. What differences can you see?

Hold your foot on the right pedal under the piano and play a few notes. Do you hear the notes echoing? This pedal is called the **sustaining pedal**. Now press the left pedal, called the soft pedal. What happens to the notes when you play them now?

This girl is playing an upright piano.

It is easy to see how a grand piano works by looking under the lid. Upright pianos work the same way, but the strings run vertically—from top to bottom. Many people have upright pianos. They are usually less expensive and smaller.

This is the inside of a grand piano. You can see three hammers hitting strings because three keys are being pressed.

The organ

The organ is often played in churches and sometimes in concert halls. It has a very loud sound that can be heard all around a large room.

In some churches and concert halls, the organ pipes cover an entire wall. When the organist plays the deep bass notes, you might feel the building shaking. It is a very exciting sound.

Look at the organ pipes in this church. They are arranged in a special pattern and are beautifully decorated.

The organ is played by pressing keys on the keyboards, called manuals, and by pressing the pedals. When a key is pressed, air is pushed through one of the pipes to produce a note. The organ is a wind instrument as well as a keyboard instrument, because air is pushed through pipes to make the sound.

There are several complete sets of pipes that produce different sounds. The two main kinds are flue pipes, which are like huge recorders, and reed pipes. In a reed pipe, a metal reed **vibrates** inside the pipe as the air passes through it.

The player can choose which manual to use. He or she can also change the sound on each manual by pulling out buttons, called **stops**, at each side.

One person can produce many sounds on the organ by using the manuals, the pedals, and different pipes and stops. Organists have to be very organized so that they can do a lot of things at once.

You could visit a local church and ask permission to watch the organist practicing.

This church organ has three manuals. Some only have two. The organist has another keyboard of pedals at his feet. These pedals play the lowest bass notes. The organist has to feel for the right pedals because he cannot see past the manuals while he is playing.

An orchestra at your fingertips

There are electronic keyboards that can sound like a whole orchestra playing. The sound of each different instrument can be produced by touching a button. This is because each instrument's sound has been recorded and stored separately in the electronic instrument's computer memory.

This boy is playing an electronic keyboard with two manuals and with buttons at the side. He can use the buttons to make different instrument sounds.

Electronic instruments do not produce their own sounds. They produce an electric sound signal that goes along a cable to an **amplifier** and loudspeaker. This is how an electric guitar works, too.

Many electronic keyboards are **synthesizers**. Synthesizers can produce new sounds as well as the sounds of "real" musical instruments. There are many ways of making exciting music, and they can all be performed and recorded by just one person!

If you have the chance to use an electronic keyboard, try out the different instrument switches such as piano, harpsichord, and organ. Do they sound like the real instruments?

This boy is trying out the different switches on an electronic keyboard. There are some switches that produce the sound of people's voices.

Choose a simple melody. Try playing it by using different voice switches, and then choose the one you like best. Now try out all the rhythm styles, and find one that goes well with your tune.

Ask a partner to play the chords while you play the tune. You may have a single finger chord switch on your keyboard. If not, look at page 26 to find out how to form simple chords.

Keyboards in the orchestra

The piano is used in some large orchestras. Sometimes, an instrument called a celesta is played.

The celesta looks like a small piano. The notes are produced by hammers that strike soft metal bars. The celesta has a very sweet sound.

This orchestra is playing a piece of music called a piano **concerto**. *The solo piano player is joined by an orchestra. The orchestra sometimes accompanies the piano, and sometimes it plays its own tunes.*

Patterns of sound

Do you know how to play a scale on a keyboard?

First, play a C on the piano. Using only the white notes, play up to the next C. You have just played a scale of C major.

A scale is a musical ladder with steps going up from the bottom note to the top note and then down again. The scale you played is one of the scales found in most western music. It is only one of the many scales played around the world.

Here is a piano keyboard. The note to the left of every pair of black notes is called C.

Scales developed from the melodies people sang. Scales are the notes that are easy to sing and are arranged as a musical ladder. The size of the step between each note is called an interval.

The scale that feels most comfortable to western ears has a pattern of tones and semitones. A tone is a whole step up on the scale. A semitone is a half step up. The note D is a tone higher than the note C. But F is only a semitone higher than E.

Now try to play some other scales, starting on different keys. You will need to use the black keys as well as the white keys.

The mouse in this cartoon has just played a scale of G major by jumping up the keyboard.

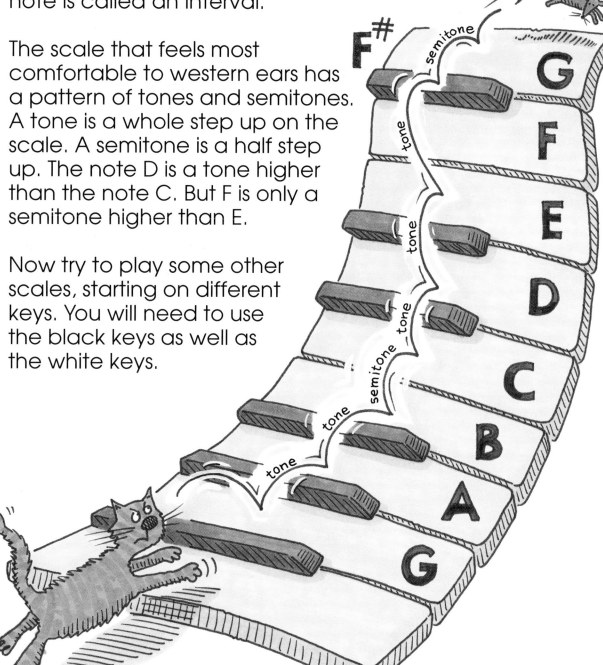

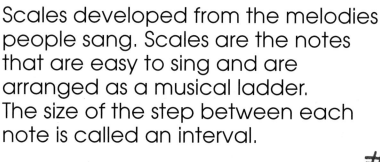

14

In harmony

Think of all the times your school piano is used to accompany singing. Your teacher plays chords that fit the melody you are singing.

Traditional music in many parts of the world is usually made up of a single melody accompanied by a rhythm instrument. There is no accompaniment based on changing chords, and different tunes are not usually played or sung together. The music is often not written down. You might have listened to Indian, Chinese, or Arabic music in this style.

This music teacher is accompanying a school choir. The accompaniment helps to keep everybody playing and singing in time together, and it adds the special sound of the piano to the music.

In the west, music has developed differently. There are usually several instruments, each playing a different part. All the parts fit together to make a rich sound. This is called playing in **harmony**. The music is written down by the composer so that the musicians know exactly what to play.

Today, composers all over the world write their music down. This composer is working on a new piece of music. He is holding his score. A score is a special book in which the composer has written down the music that each instrument should play.

Keyboard instruments were developed for western music. The pattern of notes on the keyboard allows one musician to play harmonies and melodies at the same time.

Listen carefully the next time your teacher plays the piano to accompany a song. Try singing without the piano. What difference do you think the piano makes to your music?

The girl on the left is accompanying her classmates on the piano. She adds harmonies to the violin and trumpet melodies.

Keyboards from the Past

The first keyboard instrument was probably the hydraulus, which was a kind of organ. It was invented in about 250 B.C. by a Greek engineer. Water power was used to blow air through the pipes and make the sound. The Egyptians and Romans also played similar instruments.

This picture shows an organ made in Europe in the 15th century. Electricity had not yet been discovered, so the woman on the left is using bellows to push air through the pipes.

During the 16th century, the countries of Europe were wealthy. Some people became very rich and had the money and time to enjoy making music.

Rich people often owned a virginal or a spinet. These keyboard instruments had one string for every note.

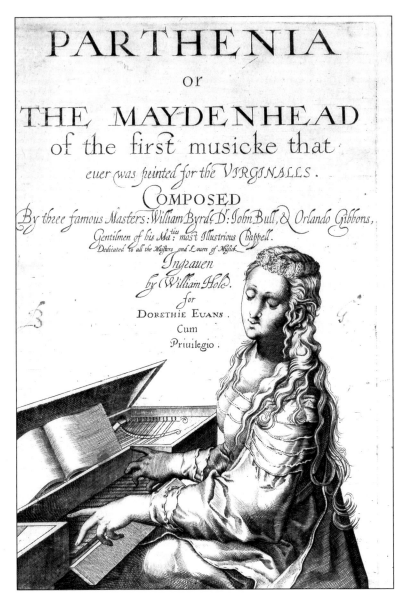

This is the cover of one of the earliest pieces of music printed for the virginal. It was printed in the early 17th century. Can you read the names of the composers?

To play a note on a virginal or spinet, the player pressed a key to operate a device called a jack. The jack plucked the string from below. Queen Elizabeth I of England was said to enjoy playing the virginal.

This is a 17th-century picture of a woman playing a spinet. Notice how short the keyboard is.

Harpsichords and clavichords

This is a harpsichord made in the 18th century. Many harpsichords were made with two manuals, one sounding a little different from the other. The harpsichord was played with orchestras and choirs, and also as a solo instrument.

During the time of the famous German composers George Frederick Handel (1685–1759) and Johann Sebastian Bach (1685–1750), the two keyboard instruments most widely used were the harpsichord and the clavichord.

The harpsichord was a larger and louder version of the spinet. It had two or more strings for each note.

At this time, much music was being written for orchestras and choirs. There were no **conductors** in those days, so the harpsichord player kept everyone playing in time together. When a harpsichord was played in this way, it was called a "continuo" because it played continuously, or all the time.

The clavichord was used in a small room for the entertainment of the player and his or her family. The sound was produced by pieces of metal, called tangents, striking the strings from below.

Clavichords were often beautifully decorated with paintings and carvings.

Harpsichord with softness and loudness

The first piano was invented in 1709 in Florence (which later became part of Italy). It was invented by Bartolomeo Christofori, who called it a *gravicembalo con piano e forte*, which means "harpsichord with softness and loudness." By the 19th century, the piano had become more popular than the harpsichord.

The piano was better than the harpsichord because it was "touch sensitive." The way the keyboard was touched could change the sound.

The Hungarian composer, Franz Liszt, playing in Vienna (now the capital of Austria). Liszt was a great pianist in the 19th century. The music he composed is very hard to play.

Try this for yourself. Play the piano softly, then loudly. Play short, jerky notes by lifting your finger as soon as you have played the note. Now play smoothly by holding each note down until you play the next one. You can do all these things on the piano but not on a harpsichord. The development of the piano allowed composers to write much more expressive keyboard music.

The piano was loud enough to be heard in large concert halls. Composers such as Mozart wrote concertos for a solo piano playing with a large orchestra.

Here is a painting of the famous composer, Wolfgang Amadeus Mozart, who lived in the 18th century. Some of his greatest works were piano concertos.

Give it a squeeze

Keyboard instruments were developed in Europe. But one of them, the harmonium, has become a very popular instrument in India. The harmonium was first brought to India by Christian **missionaries**. They used it as a small church organ.

Another kind of reed organ is the accordion. The accordion has a keyboard on the right side, and chord buttons and bass note buttons on the left. The accordionist can play both melodies and accompaniments.

The man in the middle of this Indian group is playing the harmonium. He squeezes the bellows in and out with one hand. This pushes air across metal reeds inside the instrument. The reeds vibrate to make the sound. The keyboard is played with the other hand.

The accordion is played all over Europe. You can hear it in Scottish country dance music, English morris dance music, Austrian folk music, and French café music.

The two girls at the front of this band are playing accordions. The accordion has bellows like the harmonium. To play the accordion, you have to squeeze the bellows in and out and press the chord and bass buttons with your left hand. You play the keyboard with your right hand.

Many piano accompaniments are based on chords, which may be played in different ways. The style of the accompaniment and the chords are very important in creating the mood of a piece.

Here is a way to learn to play simple chords. First, look at page 14 to remind yourself about scales, tones, and semitones.

1. The first three chords, C, F, and G major

To make a chord, you need to find the first, the third, and the fifth note of the scale. To play a C major chord on your keyboard, play C, E, and G.

C major (play C, E, G)

Now try playing a chord of F major. Play F, A, and C.

F major (play F, A, C)

To play a G major chord, play G, B, and D. Try playing with your left as well as your right hand.

You have been playing major chords. They have a bright, cheerful sound.

G major (play G, B, D)

2. The minor chords, C, F, and G
First, play C major again. Now lower the middle note of the chord, E, by a semitone. This is C minor.

C minor (play C, E♭, G)

Try the same thing with chords F and G. You will notice that minor chords have a sadder sound than major chords.

G minor (play G, B♭, D)

3. More chords

Put your hand in the position of C major. Now move your hand up one white note at a time, in the same position. Play each chord as you go. Can you hear that you are playing some major and some minor chords?

A minor (play A, C, E)

You know that you can change a major chord to a minor chord by lowering the middle note by a semitone. To change a minor chord into a major chord, you raise the middle note by a semitone. Now practice changing from one chord to another.

Piano partners

Playing **duets** with a partner is a lot of fun. Even if you haven't learned to play the piano, you could try this Twelve Bar Blues. The Twelve Bar Blues is a popular chord pattern. Player 1 plays the melody, and player 2 plays the chord accompaniment.

Twelve Bar Blues – A Duet

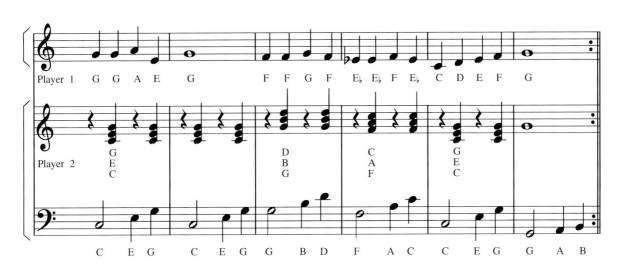

Ending

29

Glossary

Accompaniment The part played by an instrument, voice, or orchestra that accompanies the melody. It is usually played by the left hand in a piano piece.

Amplifier An electronic device used to make the sound from electric instruments louder.

Chord A group of notes that are played together to produce a good sound.

Concerto A piece of music written for a solo instrument accompanied by an orchestra.

Conductor The person who directs an orchestra or choir.

Duet A piece of music for two performers.

Harmony The playing or singing together of two or more notes to make a pleasant sound.

Melody The correct musical term for a tune.

Missionary Someone sent by a religious group to another country to persuade the people there to join their religion.

Solo The part of a piece of music that is written for just one instrument.

Stop A lever or button on an organ that is pressed to allow a set of pipes to sound.

Sustaining pedal The pedal on a piano that allows the sound of the notes to echo after they have been played.

Synthesizer An electronic instrument that can build up sounds electronically. It can imitate the sounds of instruments as well as invent new sounds.

Vibrates Shakes very quickly.

Finding out more

1. Here are some ideas for listening to keyboard music. Look for tapes, CDs, or records in your local library.

Accordion: *Piano with Braces: The Garlic and Gauloises World of French Accordionists and Singers.*

Clavichord: *Forty-eight Preludes and Fugues* by J. S. Bach.

Harmonium: *Anupjalota singing ghazals.* A well-known Indian musician singing Urdu poetry set to music.

Jazz piano: Pieces by Duke Ellington, such as *Take the A Train* and *Satin Doll.*

Piano rags by Scott Joplin, such as *Maple Leaf Rag* and *The Entertainer.*

Piano concertos: *Piano concerto No. 1 in B flat* by Peter Tchaikovsky; *Second Concerto* by Sergei Rachmaninov; *Piano concerto in C major* by Wolfgang Amadeus Mozart.

Much music has been written for piano. Listen to pieces by Beethoven, Chopin, Debussy, Haydn, and Liszt.

2. Watch your teacher play the piano, and look at the music at the same time. Ask if you can listen to a church organist practicing. Watch concerts on television. Look for keyboards and synthesizers on popular programs.

3. Try to hear some live music. Find out about recitals, local concerts for solo piano. Maybe you could watch a band rehearsing. Ask in your library for information.

Useful books

Berger, Melvin. *The Science of Music.* New York: HarperCollins, 1989.

Blocksma, Mary. *The Marvelous Music Machine: The Story of the Piano.* New York: Prentice Hall, 1984.

Greene, Carol. *Music.* Chicago: Childrens Press, 1983.

Mundy, Simon. *The Usborne Story of Music.* Tulsa: EDC, 1980.

Pillar, Marjorie. *Join the Band!.* New York: HarperCollins, 1992.

Wiseman, Ann. *Making Musical Things.* New York: Macmillan, 1979.

Index

Page numbers in **dark type** indicate subjects shown in pictures as well as in the text.

Acknowledgments

The photographs in this book were provided by: ET Archives, 23; Fotomas Index, 18,19; M. Holford, 21; J. Holmes, 16; Hulton Picture Library, 20; Hutchison (J. Hatt), 25 (above), (B. Régent), 25 (below); Impact (M. Black), 15; Link (O. Eliason), 4 and 6 (above); Mary Evans Picture Library, 22, 24; Photri (Hubatka), 10; Redferns (O. Noel), 13; Tony Stone Worldwide, 12; Wayland Picture Library, 9, 17 (Z. Mukhida), *cover*, 5, 7, 11, 26 (both), 27 (all), 28, (J. Waterlow), 7 (above); ZEFA (P. Finzer), 8; Artwork: Tony de Saulles, 14.